YOU CAN TELL THE HORSE ANYTHING

YOU CAN
TELL THE HORSE
ANYTHING

Mary A. Koncel

TP

TUPELO PRESS

You Can Tell The Horse Anything

Copyright © 2003 Mary A. Koncel

LCCN # 2003104722

First paperback edition, January 2004

ISBN 1-932195-08-4

Printed in Canada

Tupelo Press
PO Box 539, Dorset, Vermont 05251
802.366.8185 • Fax 802.362.1883
editor@tupelopress.org • web www.tupelopress.org

Cover and text designed by William Kuch, WK Graphic Design

In sweet memory of my nephew
John Robert Koncel
1999-2003

To D.W.

CONTENTS

I

II

III

IV

1

AFTER THE WEATHER

Yesterday a man was sucked out of an airplane over the blue-tipped mountains of Bolivia. He didn't cry "emergency." He didn't buzz the stewardess. He just dropped his fork, opened his mouth, and let the wind gather him inch by inch.

The other passengers agreed. This was real life, better than the movie or chicken salad. They leaned out of their seats, envying the man, arms and legs spread like a sheet, discovering raw air and the breath of migrating angels.

Below an old peasant woman beat her tortilla. She never dreamed that above her a man was losing his heart. Perhaps she was a barren woman, and, when he landed, she'd say, "Yes, this is my son, a little old and a little late, but still my son."

And the man, he thought of wind and flocks of severed wings, then closed his eyes and arched himself again. He didn't understand. His head began to ache. He understood Buicks, red hair, the smell of day-old beer. But not these clouds, this new, white sunlight, or the fate of a man from Sandusky, Ohio.

THE BIG DEEP VOICE OF GOD

That morning Tommy Rodriguez heard a voice, so he piled his family into the car and headed down the interstate. "Take off your clothes," he ordered after a while. And because Tommy had heard the voice, maybe the big deep voice of God, they all obeyed, watched shirts and underpants fly out the window, twisting and turning like strange desert birds.

Around noon, Tommy's wife began to wonder. She hadn't heard the voice but thought if she did it would call her "Sugar." "Sugar," it would say, "your thighs are hives of honey, and I am the Bumble Bee of Love." Quivering, she pressed her left cheek against warm blue vinyl.

At home, she often wondered too. There, on those late summer evenings, she leaned across the sink into still white clouds of steam and listened. Opening her mouth, she always took in more than air and water.

Tommy drove a little faster, beyond the vast and restless sand, a failing sunset, the tangled fists of tumbleweed. In the backseat, Grandpa whined, and Aunt Maria began to pee. Tommy closed his eyes. He was sure salvation was just one billboard or gas pump away, sure the voice was whispering. "Drive like the wind," it was telling him now, "like a wild saint in the Texan wind."

I stop to watch the horses in the park. Metallic and bare-boned, a whole herd of city horses. They look almost real until a boy crawls beneath the rearing one and jams an ice cream cone between its back legs.

This is why I left the city. It's no place for even these horses, and the short, sweaty man beside me is talking to his shoe. "Weather," he says, "I need some weather."

The boy runs toward his mother. Sitting on a wedge of newspaper, she eats her own ice cream cone that's dripping down her thigh. The sun is hot and beating everything into place—grass, waving mothers with Quick-Tip curlers fastened to their heads, the limp, white pedestrians and nearby traffic buzz.

I'm convinced. These horses need some hair. In the city, a little hair could go a long way. It could glisten in the sun, imbue their private parts, make them more than flat, uncomely angles and muted space. A little hair in just the right spot, and maybe I'd ease down and graze, a small-hoofed hussy.

Laughing, the boy veers off, finger raised in a slow framed obscenity. He wants the horses. His mother stands up, calling as if she could bring him back.

The conductor crawls into my lap. Resting his head against my shoulder, he sucks his thumb, rolls back his eyes, and calls me "mother."

It is times like this that I regret. I am not his mother. He is a short, bald man from Akron, Ohio. I could never sing him midnight lullabies or offer him a breast full of pure mother's milk. "Go away," I whisper in the soft, fleshy folds of his ears.

My husband returns from the bathroom, proud hips swaying with the train's steady rhythm. Unwrapping a package of cigars, he lights the thickest one and places it between the conductor's lips. "My son," he says before taking his seat next to me and the mounds of corn stalks that push and groan outside the window.

Across the aisle, a woman points a donut at us, smiles, then begins a telegram. "How perfect," she writes, "a man, a woman, and their son—the bald conductor from Akron, Ohio."

I shake my head, but my husband and the conductor agree. They stare, as if expecting me to throw open my arms and take each passenger. It's all so strange. The rumble of the train, the quiet blur of towns, this pale black halo of motherhood that looms above my head.

BUMP

When I hit a bump in the road, I never think bump. I think poor, big man lying in the middle of the road. And once again I've hit him, flattened him good, all four wheels, dead center.

I'm headed home. It's always dark. Sometimes rainy. I say, "Oh dear, not again." This poor man should be asleep in his red chaise lounge. His fried chicken dinner half eaten, and he settled in for the evening, his mother knitting beside him, a cat or two licking their tails.

I think if only it was a bump, a huge unrepentant swelling of pavement. If only, minutes before, the man told his mother, "I think I'll read a book tonight. Sit here in my red chaise lounge." A bump would be so much simpler. No pity. No remorse. And his mother so much like mine.

Now she's alone. She's wishing her son through the front door, past the telephone table, across the blue-flecked linoleum. How much he loves her chicken. Who wouldn't? Especially the wings and thighs.

Then there's the road. It's no help. "Screw the man," it tells me in the wet, raspy voice of a road. Still I bite my lip as I try to remember back, sort the bumps from the men, the men from the bumps.

WHEN THE BABIES DISCOVER TORQUE

We tell them over and over. "Babies, go to bed. Babies, wash your hands. Babies, don't drink and drive." They never listen. Inside the garage, soft heads bumping under the car hood like moths against a light bulb, they pass the tools between them. We decide to sing some nursery rhymes, remind them who they really are. "This little baby's eating spark plugs, this little baby's ripping out hoses, and this little baby's thumping tie rods—whomp, whomp, whomp." We think we should try to save them, but we're not sure from what. Torque? The sultry lure of silicone grease and deep tread rubber? Between the heavy purr and rev of engine, in the sweet, low garble of baby talk, we hear them tell us something. "Blow it out your ass." We step outside, close the door between us.

FINAL RINSE AND AGITATION

In "Timely Homestead Tips," Violet Megler of Hebron, Indiana, suggests using a bag of frozen peas to ice bad sprains while Mary Lou Becket of Stockdale, New Jersey, swears that bacon freezes better when each slice is wrapped in cellophane. No waste. No rubbery aftertaste.

At first I'm thinking theme—frozen this and thats, especially after reading how Betty Tiggins of Midvale, Idaho, lines her cooler with sheets of newspaper to keep the frozen products from thawing. Thirty-five long miles to the A & P, she sometimes drives with her husband Frank. Then I find Alberta.

I'm ready for Alberta. I'm sitting here, at the Suds & Duds Laundromat, halfway between final agitation and rinse. The man across from me is combing his hair. He smells like capfuls of fabric softener, a little too sweet and springy, and I'm tired of watching his socks and Jockey underpants tumble obscenely in the dryer.

Alberta writes about her toothbrush. All the way from Sidney, Montana. "The handle on my toothbrush gets slippery when it's wet…" Such truth, I decide. Just like mine. Just like the speckled floor of the Suds & Duds Laundromat. Or newly oiled roads after days of torrential rain.

So much danger, so much potential for disaster. Split lips. Fractured femurs. Careening 4 X 4s and school buses with pale, unconscious drivers. But not in Sidney, Montana. Three blocks east, one south, Alberta is brushing her teeth. A little Colgate and a rubber band wrapped around the brush for better grip.

It's always the pig. Not the goat, the black-bellied heifer with her wobbly calf, or the chickens with frostbitten toes. No, it's the pig running down the middle of the road, squealing those high-pitched obscenities, dust rising off its cloven hooves, and close behind, the farmer yelling back, "I'll kill you, you son of a bitch." Of course, you stop. Imagine, though, if you didn't. Imagine that you swerved, fishtailing across the road, two wheels in the gully then out and still you kept on driving. Imagine you had a daughter, Bridget or Athena, and she's covering her big bright eyes with her hands, jamming her feet into the floor, and screaming that she wished you weren't her mother because you wear ugly brown shoes, because you always drive too fast and now you've hit that pig, that poor, poor pig. A few hours ago, you were napping, sunlight cresting over your body, and now you're trying to convince her, your Bridget or Athena, that the pig is safe, you only grazed it, a little bump on the shoulder, that's all.

COME BACK, ELVIS, COME BACK TO HOLYOKE

They still love you, Elvis. They want your hair, stories about your Harley ripping up pavement between Nashville and Memphis, your sequined gaze, your big-breasted women in too-tight bikinis. "Teacher," they say to me, "Make us walk and talk like Elvis."

I tell them you're dead, fat, bloated, overweight and dead. But Juan Carlos insists that you live below him, that you stir steaming pots of black beans while singing "Maria Encantadora" on the radio every Tuesday. And Clarence calls you Father.

These boys need you, Elvis. Every day they sit, shaping their lips and grinding their hips beneath the desks. Across the room, I watch them, see little birds, baby roosters, dull-voiced peacocks with bare chests and tender white throats.

Elvis, I'm only a woman. I can't do it all. I'm only a woman, and they're asking more questions. When I stand up, they point at me, stare at the split of my skirt, the breasts beneath the sheen of my blouse.

Next time, forget the supermarkets in Denver, the trailer park in Lafayette. Come back to Holyoke. Teach these boys to be men, great manly men, men who love women, red meat, and '56 Fords. Elvis, like the streets of Holyoke, my arms wait for you, your low lean rumble.

BLACKFLIES

Morning and already a flutter of "Why's." Why onion bagels? Why a loose right turn onto Route 66 and blackflies thumping my windshield? And why is a man dressed like a chicken standing in the Big E parking lot, holding a sign that says "Why?"

Traffic is thick. It's April. Time to change the subject. So I nurse my clutch and think about the runaway hot dog cart in New York City that hit a flag pole and snapped it in two.

But here they come again. Small, unfettered like those blackflies. Why a hot dog cart and no one in the parting crowd yelling, "Save yourself, save yourself"? Why poor Mrs. Denkoff? Why her moment of calm before her empty T-strap pumps and final awe?

A school bus stutters through the intersection. The man dressed like a chicken flaps a crooked wing, waves the sign above his head. A red rubber head, bright yellow feathers, and sleepy, long-mouthed children craning outside their windows.

I blow my horn. Not for Mrs. Denkoff or hot dog carts in New York City. Not for a look, an approving gesture from the man with chicken feet and morning stubble. In this minute, there's a blackfly, maybe two, buzzing my rearview mirror, and I won't ask why. Call it salvation. Call it my moment of calm.

IT ALL MAKES SENSE TO ME

Gripping my steering wheel with one hand and adjusting the sun in my rearview mirror with the other, I welcome the hot air from the heater blowing in my face like a tropical breeze. While you, my brave copilot, plague me with inquiries about Vermont, dandruff, and Lonnie's lost appetite, I contemplate the bigger issues.

It is Tuesday afternoon, and we are lost in the streets of Greenfield. To my left, three dogs mate vociferously under a rain of oak leaves. Up ahead, duplexes, then curbs, an arc of left turns, street names as foreign as a middle thumb, and a growing darkness that perches on the treetops, big and blank.

Between frost heaves and stop signs, a voice whines across the radio, "Before I was just a man ... now I'm a real man." He has four women and a tank of high octane. It all makes sense to me. Another mailbox flashes by us. A car horn blares until my teeth begin to swell.

Years ago, a mother, twenty-three and blonde, fell in love with her clutch. With a back seat full of sheets or Cheerios, she navigated from one streetlight to another, a sort of pilgrimage to blacktop. Years ago, a pair of teenagers, Audrey and Lester, tattooed their hearts to a fender and disappeared in the soft purple roar of their engine. Now giving you, my copilot, the steering wheel, I unbuckle my seat belt, reach out the window, and embrace this vastness like a virgin cowboy.

II

LOVE POEM

Nearly midnight, a man and a woman lie in bed—the man thinking of dented hubcaps, a hand spinning out of control, breath clear as gasoline and the woman thinking of her cat.

It's nothing kinky. It's just that the cat knows how to have a good time. A fat orange tabby prowling down alleys, trash cans and doorways standing at bay as he hunts for his kind of love, a loud vernacular love. And everywhere the slight blue hum of moonlight.

The woman could easily follow, get down on all fours and leap off the windowsill, learn to arch her back like a bitch in heat. She could get used to that.

Of course, the cat is oblivious. He stops, rubs against his shadow, stretches one thick leg then another before deciding north or south. Tonight, he's looking good. After all, it's summer—flagrant stars, a toiling sky, and the smell of life moving on.

If only the man would turn. If only he would reach beneath the sheets and find the warmth of thigh. If only the man would be a man. Tired, the woman slowly drifts off to sleep. Another stupid sleep, she tells herself, the room and its darkness aching around her.

SIMPLE AS THE NIGHT

Over breakfast, I tell my friend about a woman. I tell him she's a widow, maybe 65 or 70, that she raises worms in wooden boxes filled with dirt, waters them twice a day, and on certain nights when the moon settles high above the farthest mountain, she thinks they look more like little sacs of lust than worms. It's all in her book, I tell my friend.

My friend stops eating. He agrees, this lust is everywhere. Sometimes he smells it in the crease of linen sheets blowing from a clothesline or hears it in the footsteps of teenagers walking past an opened window. He leans across me, staring down a plate of fried eggs and bacon. Yes, he says, a woman who raises worms should write a book.

It's good, I tell my friend, that this woman finds such pleasure in dirt, air, and wooden boxes, good that, at 65 or 70, she's made a life with worms and water. No husband, no dogs or children, she lives in the mountains with worms and water. Lust is simple, she writes, as simple as this night that folds itself around my ankles.

My friend shrugs. He waves his fork in front of me. We could learn a lesson from this woman, he finally says. Something about books, something about lust, past and present, something about the way our hands open or close at will.

WHEN THE BABIES FIND A CAT

We want the babies to pet the cat nicely. We show them how to scratch behind its ears, cuddle it in their soft, lumpy laps. The babies pretend to try. They hold the cat beneath its front legs, hugging it tightly. But deep down, we know they're thinking bad baby thoughts: When does a kitty learn to swim? How far can a pair of kitties be dragged by their tails? The cat swats at them, leaps for the window sill, its back arched in a rise of gray fur. We wonder if the cat can read the babies' minds. We've heard about natural instincts. The babies have their own. Outside, early each morning, they hid under shrubs with thin nylon rope and a pair of sharp scissors. "Here, Kitty, Kitty," the babies call, their faces beaming between thorny branches.

NEIGHBOR

When my horse trots across the pasture, looking somewhat lame, I think it's not her, it must be the ground, uneven, tilted ground.

Down the road, just a few rocks and duck flags away, the fat woman is leaning too far back in her chair. Her husband stands by the sink, holding on, but she's too angry, leaning too far back. So much anger—the fat woman punching air, pulling out spitcurls, and the kitchen floor tipping up, creaking around her.

My horse snorts and slides to a halt. When the ground is uneven, it's hard for a horse to flex its hocks, step long and hungry, match stride for stride. It's hard because the fat woman is leaning back, yelling something about potatoes—- a sudden, fitful memory.

Her husband, afraid for the teapot, the bird bath splashing over, daffodils uprooted from their own, tries to calm her. "Darling," he begs her, "darling."

Sweet words. Sweet ground. How easily I want both. One wafting up, lost between the trees, the chunks of broken clouds, the other flat and green beneath my horse.

WHAT WOULD MARTHA STEWART SAY?

In the red brick bungalow, the woman is pouring a fifth of bourbon over her husband's head. She's tilting the bottle, steadying it above him, he's sitting in his La-Z-Boy, bare feet glistening, lap pooled, overflowing with bourbon.

If the woman had some shampoo. If she could learn to find comfort in the bubbles and bourbon, a slip of pleasure in her husband's round awkward head. If she could ask him to lean back, smile, then remind him again. He forgets. He's old. He wants crushed ice with his bourbon.

The woman won't stop pouring until the last drop. She wishes she had another bottle. Scotch. Vodka. A hearty French cognac, aged for months in real wood barrels. She just wants to pour something wet and bitter over her husband, a sort of do-it-yourself baptism, a spontaneous cleansing. Better late than never. That's what the woman is thinking.

Her husband raises a hand, wipes his eyebrows. He could tell the woman to stop right now. He could be insistent, maybe even take a swing. After all, she's his wife, and it is his bourbon, his damned bourbon.

RED DOOR

A horse grazes outside a red door. Occasionally he lifts his head and listens to the voices behind the door, two voices that whisper about apples, oak chairs, the last pale breath of winter.

Inside, a man and woman sit. They have watched the horse for hours, come to love the slow toss of his mane, the strong black curve of his back. If asked, the man would say the horse was a handsome horse, but the woman would not reply. She would stand, brush crumbs from her waist, maybe stir a pot of stew, its raw steam filling the awkward spaces.

Will he take her hand? How long can she wait? Will they turn to each other before they give themselves to sleep? These are the questions the horse would like answered. Last year he wondered about damp morning grass and scattered streams. Now he just wants to know about the red door and the man and woman behind it.

Yes, the woman thinks, it is time to believe. She leans against the man who catches her shoulders and strains to see the horse. But in what, she asks, her voice almost growing loud, as if there was an answer, as if the man or horse would care.

The horse reaches toward another clump of clover, tearing off leaf then flower. He is nearly full. Above him, clouds edge across the sky and starlings settle deep in distant hemlocks. The horse looks up, shifts from one hoof to another, feels the weight, he is almost certain, of something.

LUCY'S THOUGHTS ON WEDNESDAY

"I thought I'd lend him my car so maybe
he could look for a job or something.
Instead he spent the whole day stalking a girl."

At Jimbo's Package Store, Lucy stands behind the counter, polishing her nails a shade deeper. Above her, a fan spins smoothly. "So tell me," she says to Timmy because he wears leather boots, because she thinks he can bully truths about her brother from the bottom of that freezer.

Timmy pops open another Bud. He swallows hard, lowers his jaw. "A man's got to do what a man's got to do," he explains, lips wet and urgent as the words between them.

Sunlight tumbles across speckled linoleum. In aisle three, a woman caresses Playtex gloves as if they were a poodle. "Good, good," she sings, tucking them into her purse, plump legs already dancing home where she'll bleach tomato stains and love a man with little hair.

Lucy has no man. Today, this Wednesday, there's only a brother who drives down long, compliant roads in a fast blue car with reinforced fenders.

And, of course, Timmy. Lucy waves her nails into the air, watches him rub labels into tiny spitballs. Flicking them off, he settles himself. "So tell me," she says again because she needs to know why one man speaks slow and gravelly, why another chooses big-haired blondes and absolute undergrowth.

ON THE 50TH ANNIVERSARY OF D-DAY
STELLA LONGS FOR LOVE

"The average age of the paratroopers is 72."
Associated Press

This Monday, as Stella irons sheets and beats bread dough against red Formica, she's longing for love. On the television, across the other ocean, old men are leaping out of planes, fingers groping foreign air, sunlight warming fluttering cuffs, slow but arrogant bones.

In the corner, Alice watches too. She watches Stella step over and touch the soft, swarthy cheeks of a distant man, whispering, "That one, that one can jump start my heart." Alice nods, pushes crumbs of coffeecake around her plate, and remembers her Freddie's steamy young thighs.

The old men breathe deeply, forgetting the first lesson of fear. One by one, they lean over, open themselves, drift vaguely, east then west. Fifty years ago, an ocean slammed beneath them, and the whole world hunkered down for the big one. Now this sky of sheer white clouds, seagulls, a breeze as bare and sudden as mercy.

"Anything's possible," Stella wants to tell Alice. His name is Thomas. He sells leather shoes or paperclips in Poughkeepsie and drives through winter storms, left arm dangling out the window. And always, behind a platter of string beans and a well-salted pork roast, Stella waits, her apron blooming.

ERMA JACOWITTS PLEADS HER CASE

Last night my husband rolled over and yelled, "Erma, go feed those chickens." Not once, but twice in a voice so loud the shutters nearly turned on the wall.

It was 3:22. I knew because I looked at the clock, then thought we have no chickens. They died last spring. All fourteen. I usually ignore my husband, but last night I cursed him widely. I called him names not fit for a roadhouse whore. He has no respect for me or the dead.

Believe me when I say this. I've watched him sleep. There's evil on his breath. His mouth drops open, and his chest heaves up and down as if it couldn't stop. Sure, I listen, look at something that isn't there, think bad thoughts.

When my husband woke up, he didn't remember. He said, "Erma, where's my coffee?" I could have thrown sugar at him—told him to stuff those chickens between his legs. But I didn't. They died last spring. It was a damp, rude day, the kind that falls somewhere in the middle of each week.

When Norma woke up, she was standing in the parking lot, a bag of French fries in her hand and neon lights spilling letters down her shoulders like a brilliant waterfall or something just as big.

"Norma," I called, "where's the catsup?" But what I really wondered about was the car, her nightgown soft as breath, and the moon air that pulled her from our bed and into the streets.

Every night I waited for Norma to abandon herself to that moment of sleep. Behind the headlights, she became a real night angel with velvet dice, fenders, and a strong southern wind. Sometimes I followed her, watched her move between the curbs and alleys as if they were rooms in our house, then caught her just before she went too far. And sometimes I just drank, dreaming about a man and his woman with the thin, faithful ankles.

Afterwards, Norma never explained, and I never asked. But I had my thoughts. I called it hunger. Not for the flesh of a new man. Not for slow dance in tight, dimly lit corners. But a hunger for something that she couldn't speak but grew too large when she closed her eyes and gave her body to blacktop.

"Norma," I called again, "save some for me." As she turned, I remembered her hair, the way it twisted, long and leisurely, across her forehead like a crown or borrowed halo. Sure, I wanted her then. Sure, I wished she wanted me.

TALK

You can tell the horse anything. You can tell him about the weather, fancy lace underpants, bored neighbors with fat tender stares. The horse will listen. He'll ease himself into the corner of the stall, flick back an ear, scratch a leg, or toss through his hay. In the pasture, summer wafts between the fence posts, and clover is blooming again. But the horse will stay. You can tell him about your head, how it aches when you see bare trees and remember a red-haired child, pale and breathless in her shadow. The horse'll nod. He will listen as you untangle his forelock, rub his belly, feed him a handful of sugar cubes and maybe a pear. You can tell him that nothing matters to you, nothing. Oh horse, you'll whisper, because you are so happy, because the day is long, and the horse is snorting.

SOMETHING LIKE THE EARTH

In corn country, we watch the corn grow. A simple task, and tomorrow will be no different. Sitting, we reshuffle our ankles, nod toward the field, each row delicately parted.

We know how to live, what to expect from a bare summer breeze, when to relish that sullen growth. Once, in the back forty, lured from a flatbed Chevy, a boy and girl tangled, rubbed themselves in root and broken stalk. He turned whispering. She tugged loose her braid. And then the muffled rapture.

It always comes back to corn...

We've learned our lessons well. Respect the dirt, the sun and rain. Respect the seed and the farmer rising from morning sheets, arms stretched, broad chest already heaving with the promise of sweat and sudden ache.

Outside, on a crook of oak limbs, crows perch, wait, heads turned in their well-fastened hoods. Sometimes they rustle, wings burning under a dazed sun, before the farmer empties his cup and laces each boot.

Outside the kitchen window, the smelly foot tree is blooming again, a mob of bumble bees circling its extravagant, but smelly white blossoms. For years, I mistakenly turned to my husband. "Put on your shoes," I implored him. "Change your socks. Wash your feet."

How easily the smelly foot tree can make us forget those we love. In the throes of spring, as daffodils and tulips tussle in the ground beneath us and the breeze, complacent in its dirty little deed, lifts and carries the scent of that tree, how easily we blame.

Across the road, there's no smelly foot tree. Only an oak, two maples, one drooping with songbirds, and a patch of bright sumacs that aren't really trees. Imposters, my husband and I called them in better times.

In that yard, the new wife happy as her unwrapped peonies, and the husband even happier as he digs through the compost heap, his red wheel barrel full, overflowing.

Once I almost wrote an ode. "Oh tree outside the kitchen window," I began, "small woody wonder of nature." But I stuttered, struck by the sway of its branches, the breadth of its treeself. It was almost spring, and I, too, was young.

I've learned the difference. Some trees are kind. I point to them, call them good trees—trees that lavish us with shade, overripe fruit, squirrels, the righteous mingling of roots. Others are bad, rude trees, trees of endless bird droppings.

So I say this aloud. To myself and my husband, to the bland, the innocent strolling three blocks down, their cheeks as smooth and joyful as fat wet beagles. Forgive me. But beware. Beware of spring, its warm undulating urges.

EDDIE'S MOTORS

Eddie loves the swell of spring. He waves sparkplugs in my face, tells me how he alone can teach them to bloom like a field of frantic iris.

If we were alone, I would call him "God," "Lord," "Master of my Fervent Soul." I would find new faith under his bulging black fingernails, then rev it up and surrender it back, skidding turbocharged.

But his Snap-On girls are watching. They've heard it all before. Eddie's using the lingo, Eddie's measuring each gesture while I stand here agog, a wobbling mortal in this sanctum of fan belts, sleek twisting hoses, steel-belted radials all pumped for performance.

An hour ago, I was stuck, stranded, puddle water lapping against my fenders, across my engine. Other men came and went, hearts pressed to steering wheels, hands too weary to behold this new cacophony of landscape, this air bright and jubilant as the faces of newborn calves.

Eddie came, Eddie saw, Eddie saved. This man with a tow truck could hold back this whole tide of season or pop it open like a 12-pack of Valvoline, let it ooze, sweet and southerly, between our intertwined toes. And me, I think I'll swoon again, loving torque and utter brawn.

THE YEAR OF THE MAN

My friends aren't hungry anymore. When they walk down streets, they belch and rub their fat, slick bellies. "You, you, and you," they say, pointing their fingers as if sorting Buicks from Fords, left feet from right ones.

These men are looking pretty good. And it's not even spring. It's the year of the man. Before it was a drought, a drought on top of a drought. Now they're dropping from trees, sprouting through cracks, littering parks and alleys like empty bottles or dented cans.

And my poor, poor husband! Every night he dreams he's a windswept virgin stranded on a ragged cliff in some dark, undeclared country. "What does it mean?" he asks me. "What does it mean?" I tell him about the sad old days, about big vacant beds and the song of the drought, that long, long drought. And always, of course, I tell him, "Sure, I want you, I need you," over and over.

Last week even Peggy called me. Whispering, "It smells a little fleshy today," she abruptly hung up. I stepped out on my porch and breathed, letting beads of sweat and full ripe muscles fill my lungs. "Yes," I wrote back three days later, "the sweet still scent of thigh."

EMANUEL ON THE TIGHTROPE

In this small corner, snow drifts higher than the last flock of swallows, and the wind beats cherry trees as if they were cheap tin drums. But 1,200 miles south, in the big city, a man sits on a tightrope, eating cheese sandwiches and watching a television strapped to his wrist.

His name is Emanuel, and, 600 feet above sidewalks and cigarette butts, lawn mowers and potted palms, he's no longer a man with a dozen lug wrenches and a weary blonde wife. He's the man on the tightrope.

I know the truth. Today, as I shiver again while another round of winter pounds on my front door, repeating, "You, you, you." I know that this man is afraid of the earth. I am sure of this as I am sure that sky and lake can freeze together, that February follows January like a well-trained mutt, and that this man too has shuddered in his sleep.

Emanuel blows kisses to the crowd below. "It's a dream," he tells them, "the dream of a real, everyday man." He turns away from the sun that drags itself across the horizon, straightens his shoulders, and waves two fingers as if they were his flag.

Up there, he is safe. Yet all over the earth, people are shrinking back. Wrapped and huddled, they think of Emanuel growing taller, his bare chest catching last night's drizzle of stars. "Hold on, Emanuel," we whisper through our clenched right fists. "Hold on."

It has to stop. These farmers are too old. Still they go into their fields to burn back the brush, burn off the stumps and disease that make this soil too harsh and heavy. Instead they burn themselves.

I blame asparagus. All of these farmers grew asparagus. One died holding a rake in his hands, a bitter circle of flames taking his mouth, his hair, his arms and legs, but not his rake. "He got too excited," a good neighbor insisted. "These old men see fire and get too excited."

Then there's Mr. Clark. At 82, he had been burning for 58 years. That morning his wife scrubbed pots and dreamed about asparagus. She dreamed about late spring passing into summer, its damp, cool mornings and patches of lean asparagus while her husband danced alone in the fire. Left foot forward, right foot out, he stumbled and finally let himself be taken.

This man—a kind, old man—just wanted to give his wife asparagus like he gave himself to her so many nights. That morning he burrowed his hands into the soil, cleared his throat for words that would turn seed into swollen stalks, and almost knelt for one minute before striking his match.

I need to know. When did this farmer learn to dance so well? When did these farmers forget that fire always takes more than it needs? Or did they simply think, once and for all, "Too much spring, too much asparagus." Then, backs pressed against field and horizon, did they think about wings, the wrinkled tips of angel wings.

FALLING

As Sister and Baby tumbled from the window, they never thought poorly of Mother. Mother will catch us, they lipped to one another. Mother catches everything. Surely she'll be waiting, standing tiptoe, arms stretched wide for Sister and Baby.

Coughing, the man on the tenth floor poured straight tea and spooned his oatmeal. Ask him and he'll swear he saw angels, wingless angels careening down, in red cartoon pajamas, even if it wasn't Christmas, wasn't late near midnight when any slow, unfolding shape can break from the sky.

Make no mistake. Mother knew the difference between children and angels. Angels don't scream riddles. They don't scrape their heels or pound their empty bowls. Remembering, Mother looked down and twirled more hair against her cheek.

But the man was so certain. On the tenth floor, between the roof and courtyard litter, he could expect falling clumps of begonias, the mute but ardent drift of season, pigeons fat and feathery as angels. "Goddamned pigeons," the man insisted to himself again. "Goddamned angels."

Sister and Baby never opened their eyes, never saw Mother push back from the window. They fingered the air. Lovely air, thought Sister as Baby rocked gently above her, head over feet.

MAYBE IT'S STILL WINTER

I've vowed to end this year on a blank note, an empty page that unrolls down the sidewalk, mile after desolate mile. My husband tries to remind me of something, anything. "You emptied the trash just yesterday," he insists. But I've regressed to summer, a sticky Thursday night, my friend refusing to kiss the Elvis impersonator after he leaned across me and three seats of other women in pink florescent T-shirts. He wanted a cheek. She offered a hand. Next day, he was riding his motorcycle and lost his left leg. I've forgotten most of the details. See, I'm getting quite proficient. If I press my fingers tips hard against my temples, last April becomes a comfortable blur. I hardly remember the cat's belly growing too large, my hay drenched and moldy, the neighbor couple swearing behind the lilac bushes as I try to talk to my brother on the telephone, his voice too soft. He tells me he's tired. I tell him I'm sorry. Two months before that, maybe it's still winter. Maybe snow covers the sunflower seeds on the tray of the bird feeder, and I'm walking to the car, dog straining on the end of a leash.

WHEN THE BABIES ARE MISSING AGAIN

We don't even look for them. We're tired. It's Friday night, and across the living room, the man on the TV stares at us, past everyone, at us. "It's 11 o'clock. Do you know where your babies are?" We shake our heads, shrug. No. When the babies are missing, they won't be found. They wear leather jackets, sometimes wool caps. They drink, smoke, hunker behind telephone booths or trees, kiss with open lips and fat baby tongue. (They've whispered this to us. When they're home. When they've tucked themselves in blankets, sucking their thumbs, eyes rolling back with incoming sleep.) "Damn those babies," we want to say, but we don't dare. The man on the TV waits, his mouth a pink shade of expectation, a puff of disbelief. What can we tell him? That the babies hardly ever swear. That they eat their bowls of green beans and squash. We think, How to begin.

THE HEADACHE

Once headaches were banned.

In ancient caves, no reference to migraine, sinus, aspirin, or pounding, throbbing pain. Only drawings of big lovely heads with hats.

After the Flood came the first headache. Noah couldn't speak the pain, didn't know the word. So he stood, vague and mute on a rock, lusting for the ease of the Ark as morning waves lapped his withered, sun-browned toes.

My head hurts today. I ate a banana, admired hubcaps and wheel wells, brushed away fleas, and read some poems. "In the deeps there is a little bird," Frank O'Hara wrote. And there, between my ears, in the gully of my neck, the beating wings.

It hurts like a maple tree, leaves and branches, crashing on pavement, then crashing again.

It hurts like the sting of a hundred honey bees pissed at their two-bit queen who promised a field of narcissi but delivered New Jersey.

It hurts like hell, and I'm the only one left shoveling.

In the barn, the farmer is holding his head. All around him the beauty of hay, cow bellies, wooden buckets of promise and seed.

The woman walking the beagle is lucky. Varicose veins, she explains, little rampant rivers swelling up and down her thighs, but her head soft and dreamy as a cream puff.

TALKING BACK

I'm mad at a dead person for not closing the door.

I'm mad at a dead person all day today and probably tomorrow.

I'm mad at a dead person because instead of eating macaroni and cheese, I'm pulling out forsythia bushes and digging dirt that's too hard.

I'm mad at a dead person. Not angry, but mad. If someone asked, "What's the difference?" I'd say, "Here's a bottle of wine. There's a bottle of scotch."

I'm mad at a dead person for calling too often.

I'm mad at a dead person for not listening. Night after night, my voice lost in heavy breath and the blare of corner TV.

I'm mad at a dead person for not making the bed.

I'm mad at a dead person because two of my friends let their men beat them in driveways. Miles apart but their vague bodies still dropping together, shoulder then head, gravel and cheek, blood.

I'm mad at a dead person for naming a cat Tess.

I know it's not right to be mad. A dead person can't feel cold, the petulant shift of shade. A dead person can't taste, insist "eat more," point a sticky finger.

I'm mad at a dead person, and I can't remember the last time I wasn't.

I'm mad at a dead person because two dogs are circling the driveway, and I'm tired of dogs, their impossible tails.

I'm mad at a dead person.

I'm mad at a dead person for not proving me wrong.

ANOTHER POEM FOR THE DEAD

In New Orleans, our tour guide knows the dead. He tells us about wall ovens, 6 x 6 tombs with layers of family—mothers and brothers, the few shyest cousins and big old Aunt Phoebe. We're afraid of him. "Don't Piss Me Off," written on his T-shirt. "I've Run Out of Room to Bury the Bodies."

Admit it. All around us, the dead are piling up. And there we are, standing between terracotta pots of wilted petunias, eating pulled pork and sipping Budweisers, our memories insistent, and we confusing being graceful with grateful.

Our tour guide could tell us the difference. But we're just visitors in this city of beads and feathered masks. He pats the slab door of each oven, his ring finger as thick as his thumb. After one year and one day, the body is fully baked. Like Good & Dandy Chicken, he explains, extra crispy with bits of white bone. His name is Christian. He doesn't cut us any slack.

Back home, according to the maps, every small dirt road leads to a cemetery. On the right, oak leaves mingle above a creek, and loose dogs leap over headstones, noses damp and shimmering, red tongues dangling from their mouths. We drive slow, call it country living.

BRAKE FOR MOOSE

It could save your life. On a jagged road in some backwoods state when you're driving home, taunted and bruised by another lost day. Stars flick off your windshield, and the bigness of the night surrounds you.

Then along the bend, in a hollow where darkened trees and fog weave incestuously, how suddenly you think moose, see moose. Tonight you don't pass in stuttered silence, missing its blunt knees, heavy breath, belly full of leaves and twiggy vines. Tonight you just brake, brake good and hard.

No matter if the car swerves, if the road rears up and away, throws you off like an overwrought dream. You brake because you love bare swept floors, vast undulating views, your beloved sleeping in the folds of a summer sheet, the front yard crows, sullen but constant.

Nearby, at the Flat Top Diner, Hilda and her two best patrons peel themselves from the window. Before she would splatter coffee in your crotch. No napkin, no cream. Now Hilda marvels and spins your legend over the Tenderfoot Special. "Lover of Life," she will begin, "The One Who Braked, Braked Good and Hard."

And the moose, not turning or waking, lumbers back to its trees, its green and muddied undergrowth. Tucked away, it will remember you, small but vibrant in your passing.

HORSE

The old man is in the barn again. He's trying to steal my horse. 5:45 in the morning. Even the floorboards are swollen with sleep. Stumbling, he curses his knees, bales of hay, confuses flecks of moon with knotted mane.

So much always goes wrong. The old man falls out of bathtubs. Last week he peed in his bed, puddle of urine swirling over needlepoint iris, lifting their petals, then cascading down like a little Niagara. Now he's in the barn.

The old man kicks at the stall door, pulls at the latch. It's stuck in the dark, won't open, jammed up, another goddamned door. My horse lowers her fat white eyelids, ignoring him, the dark between them.

Not long ago, his wife begged me, Take him. Take him for good. He still wore shoes. I tried to say yes, imagine him cantering over snow or tumbled leaves, face pink, not losing his stirrups, not wanting.

Swallows stare down from the rafters then fold their angled wings. The old man wipes his knuckles, tinge of blood against his trousers, waiting for me, first light, the deep waking nicker of horse.

VACATION

I'm already missing my dogs, longing for tail and ecstatic wet tongue, as I try to ignore the woman standing on the ledge beside me. She's waving her arms, her small tanned hands that should be sweeping across this bay to snow-topped mountains, sailboats, sea lions bumping into dumb blue waves. All this beauty, she should be saying. Almost too much. But instead her dog took a leap, and the man below us is paddling in circles, lifting the water as if he were spooning a bowl of chicken soup, searching beneath and around it for noodles, a bit of carrot or meat. He's thinking stupid woman, I'm thinking poor woman. It's vacation, an island of friendly, happy people with crooked porches and slow rusting trucks.

At home, my dogs are sleeping on the couch, snoring or licking some private part. But her dog took a leap—a splash of fur—and the man below us is angry. So the woman wants her dog, dead or alive. So the woman has no children, can't carry the dog back to them. So the woman ignored the signs...

DANGER

STEEP CLIFFS

RESTRAIN YOUR CHILDREN AND DOGS

The man would add "Stupid" in huge block letters, maybe draw the woman into him, brush away her hair, whisper "Stupid, Stupid" in her ear. Today's no vacation for him, no tenderness. He's wishing he could leave this island. Just a short trip, a night away, no cold blunt water, he and his body still, not drifting.

MEDITATION ON A BIRD SITTING
ON A MAN'S HEAD

Not really. It's about the man. He's sleeping on a bench, beneath some leaves and a scorched morning sky. The bird is big, a pigeon perhaps. As the man lifts a hand across his cheek like a wing, children squat in a water fountain, and a red sun beats above him. No wonder he's dreaming of birds.

In some countries, a sleeping man and his bird are considered good luck. The man is woken up, given a robe, a stick, and three barrels of corn. After the bird is captured and dressed like a boy child, the man repeats the Dream of the Bird in foreign tongues.

This man's dream begins with damp feathers. His friends call him Omar, Om for short. After circling mounds of shifting sand, he swoops down and grabs a fish from the shoulder of a well-wrapped peasant. He eats, hungry for bone but not remembering pebbles or their dabbling streams.

And later? Who knows. Wind and a coarsely uttered song?

The man rolls over, mumbles into his sleeve. This summer has been long, and the bird is pecking through his hair. Poor man. Poor, tired sleeping man, lips drawn, eyes fluttering behind crusted lids as if measuring distance, discovering nest.

THE SECOND SONG OF INSOMNIA

A stranger is humming outside my window. He looks like my dead uncle or a drunk angel in rubber boots and a baggy wool overcoat. I'm just not sure. I'm easily confused by that black spot of moustache that shimmers in the half moon air.

But every night this stranger follows me home. He leans against the tree, taking for granted my grass, the staggered line of streetlights, this curtain that separates me from a deep husky sleep. Now he's rolled up his sleeves. I watch his lips, but he's too clever, his mute breath lingering inside my head like a dream, like a bad dream running over and over.

It's not right for a stranger to be humming outside my window. He should go home. He should read books, big red books, and let me close my eyes.

Listen. I need words, even simple words. I won't apologize. I want a song, a really nice song, with words that grab my heart and swing it dizzily around this room, then drop me into some midnight abyss. Instead I find myself pressed between these sheets, throat aching in my hands, waiting for the first howl of a hungry dog, the rise of footsteps, something that brings night closer to day.

WHEN THE BABIES READ *THE BOOK*
OF THE DEAD

We can't stop them. We say, "Babies, don't turn the page."
But they try to sound out every word, gum each corner until
it's soft and sticky. We say, "Babies, look here—Winnie the
Pooh, Tigger, a monarch butterfly wafting over a bed of red
and white petunias." The babies ignore us. They huddle
together, drool across the cover. They like the pictures best—
trees, man and shaggy dog together, the long, rocky trek
against time. We try to distract the babies, tickle their round
cherry chins, but they're relentless. Their fingers, eyes,
mouths, every bit of them so little but relentless. Sometimes
we think the babies might not be ours. We could ask them, but
we're afraid. The babies don't sleep at night. We hear them
rocking upstairs beneath the crib, the book held between them
like another prayer. We don't know who to call.

VIGIL

We follow the old woman outside. Snow, brittle sky, the heavy sag of winter trees. The news is not good. She is dead. The old woman hurries away. We need to tell her the news, put it to her gently. Stumbling over rocks, crusted ground, she disappears like a burst of wings on a flat, undisturbed morning. Or is it night? No matter now. We wait, wondering about the bitterness, flesh and bone. Then, between the river and frozen thicket, we see the edge of shadow, a scarf wrapped tightly. We try to lure her back with prayer. After all, she's dead. She should love our weary voices. When the old woman turns, we catch her, cradle her down. She kicks and bites us. She loses her shoes. Still we hold her quiet, kissing each hand and repeating how the body betrays so unlovingly.

DEAD HORSE

The slow pitch of the shovel. And dirt—black, warm and weary from its own weight—piled in full, heaping mounds. As if the ache in our arms was still and final.

We are digging a hole. Who would have thought? When a horse dies, legs stiffen and eyes stare at vigilant angels and clouds pushed against a faint, but stubborn horizon. This horse is dead. A kind, old, patient mare.

We raise our shovels and dig the hole. It will take the horse and all her bones. It will smother, then soothe her with its black warmth, keep her back straight, her head from raising up, fill her eyes until they close. Big, ponderous eyes, like the stretch of uncut meadow, a flock of starlings, circling.

Sometimes the hole is too deep. Sometimes it takes too much of what needs to be remembered—a flush of mane, long easy strides on muddy mornings, the press of small body against large. We stop, turn aside, trying to hold back all that needs to stay.

ON WEEPING ICONS

Across Sheffield Avenue, another bus pulls up. My mother greets the hordes of faithful, ushers them up the stairs, presses them into deep wooden pews. Today the lampata is especially bright, and Mary is weeping inside a dingy red church on the near north side of Chicago.

I ponder this. As I walk across my pasture, between another spring and fat ponies kicking through the last morning hour, I think about fence posts and weeping icons. "They're hungry for tears," my mother writes. "They want their miracles—hair, plump babies, a tide of untouched sleep."

Her job is simple. Taking the old babas first, she folds them into the small nest of her arms, carries their fleshy souls to Mary. Together, they are grateful. Now there are lips softened by sturdy prayer, incense warming the vestibule.

The children must be taught. Their knees are pink and restless. They forget how to cross themselves. Like the stern, but loving fists of God, my mother is always patient. She explains again why Mary, Theotokas, Virgin Mother of this Befuddled Earth, has given herself in streams of tears.

Sometimes I too am hungry. And I still remember how to kneel, fold my fingers and cross myself, right to left. But this morning, Mother, you should know that tall trees flicker, taut and certain, that bare, wild hooves can rise up as if in blessed flight.

It's almost like heaven out here. Ten miles of angel-pin turns, glittering blacktop, then a pair of straight yellow lines leading to sweet soul of opossum, twin spirits of skunks.

Driving home, I think about Saint Francis, imagine him wandering through the woods, a flock of swallows buzzing his left eardrum, a raccoon or two draped over his shoulders like a favorite cardigan. A tall, awkward man, he had hands with white palms and strong straight fingers.

Out here, under these brooding stars and stark moon, animals are just as abundant. Cut loose from fur and body, they languish along the road: rabbits begin to hurry but stop in mid-air, a fox sniffs its blood, surprised by its cold, exquisite beauty, while tree frogs swallow deep, vaguely tasting the last sounds in their throats.

"Keep still," Saint Francis would warn if he walked among these animals. "Keep still." One hand pressed against his lips, the other held in blessing, he would stop at each one that raised its head and wanted more.

I could stop. I could stop, drop to my knees, and hold out my hands like Saint Francis, tell these animals that they have been good, good and wild. It's time to surrender their hearts to me, their long and mournful howls, their hunger. Bless this night, bless this road and all that makes it heaven.

IV

TREE MAN

And what of the man dangling in my tree, feet barely touching air, ropes tied to the last twist of trunk? One cut here, another there, he swings wide, easing himself limb over limb.

The man is an expert. He knows the story of trees, the moist white flesh beneath their bark. If I asked, he could tell me why my horses are running wild, ears perked, hooves pounding out the shapes of danger, why wind swirls dark around them.

Ropes tightened, then knotted like a fist. I watch him, listen. When my tree falls, the sun will not break into a pile of stale red ash, my house will still be a small shuttered house. When my tree falls, I will breathe real breath. He has promised me this.

These are his words. Sick trees must surrender. Old trees must be delivered. I chant them to myself, my horses. Dust deepens the half circles of their eyes. We have nothing to lose. Not leaf, not root, not the long melodic growth of shade.

HOW I FIND ACHE EVERYWHERE

Along the gravel road, up the last hill with a hand-carved sign, Free Manure, past the shaded lot just between the split rail fence and ponies, their stout white bodies and buried heads. This morning. And again tomorrow. Next to the woman holding the pot of fancy pink petunias, two rings on one finger, a tattooed or bruised knuckle. She's saying there should be a price, please just check, $2.99, I'm sure. She's desperate for the small red tag, for her daughter in the stroller, 2-years-old, blonde, round beautiful mouth full of raisins. Ache is there. In line. After the telephone rings, the pause, the voice of the brother now barely a whisper. After midnight. After the fifth flight with rows of empty seats and an unsettled moon. Around that same time, about the time when the TV turns blank, just in time. Ache is there, waiting. While the old dog digs a hole, dirt flying between its back legs, the hole getting bigger, and something never touched, never rendered lush or impossible, lost. Even though it's May, the scent of wild strawberries almost ready. Muddy rocks.

TAKE YOUR TIME

Just a few questions. Simple ones. You don't have to answer. Just nod your head. Move your eyes. I understand. Can you remember the first day? Were you planting something yellow, rocks and old leaves clumped together, your fingernails bitten down and black? I like pansies. I think it was spring. But I should ask you. Was it spring? What do you think? About plain letters or the blink of an eye? About lines, the one that's been crossed? About strangers, the remarkable passing of the little one a curtain away, your brother? Have you come to think of me as a brother? Tell me. I want to know. Am I sitting too close? Do you miss the loveliness of horse? Have you ever thought how the body falls into sleep? Do you sleep? Do you still love Mickey Mantle? Take your time. Please feel free to answer everything or nothing at all. May I sit even closer?

Leading the horse, the girl throws off her hat and opens her mouth, lets snow cascade between her lips. The horse stumbles behind, aware of its shiver, its deep blunt hoof prints. It wants its barn, corner of hay, chickens warmly rooted in their nests. But tonight the girl is walking in circles, behind two rocks, around a vigilant pine tree, not to the barn, but in another circle beneath long branches and folded wings. The girl sticks out her tongue, catching more snow. "River," she calls out, meekness of snow inside her. The horse can only follow, feeling numb, as it tosses its mane, flattens its ears. Long ago, it might have reared up, maybe stomped the girl, one hoof breaking cheekbone into splinters, red and fiercely cut.

NAMING ACHE

I begin with the obvious. Heartache. But Ache says no. Wants something more subtle.

I say I'm tired. Enough for tonight.

I say it's hard to name Ache, even harder to live with Ache, weeks then months, driving, stopping for cheeseburgers, waiting in the supermarket, 12 items or less, scrubbing the kitchen floor, each corner twice.

Now it's Tuesday.

I slept, walked this way and that, showered in the dark. I try again. I'm thinking nickname. Something familiar. Personal. Like Stumpy. Instead of saying, I wish this Ache away, I could say, Go lie down, Stumpy. Or Look, Stumpy, it's time to hit the road.

I'm growing fond of Stumpy, almost feel like I could pet Stumpy, cuddle on the couch. I could plant giant yellow zinnias, read another chapter of *Tender Is the Night*. All for Stumpy. But Ache is insistent. Says no. Wants something that resonates. Something about the baby, the horse, the fat friend.

I say too bad. I'm hungry. It's dinnertime. The string beans are hot, and the table set. But Ache is waiting. I say How about Pain in the Ass. I say it loud. Refuse to say Constant Ache, Ache Too Much, Unbearable Ache.

Ache says fine. Let's eat.

WHEN THE BABIES ARE HUNGRY

We could try to feed them, give them bottles of milk or grape juice, promise to swing them over our shoulders and pat their backs until they belch. Then again, why bother? The babies won't eat. They sit around the kitchen table, staring at spoons, their mouths pretending to chew. Opening and closing, but always empty. We watch them from behind the counter. Wonder. They think they can annoy us, teach us a lesson or two about hunger when they hold their heads and rub their flat pink bellies. But we know they're just babies. We know they'll get hungry. Tonight. Tomorrow. We can wait. Then we'll tell them a little story of our own. It begins in a nearby town. In a house like this one, with a wide lush garden, lovely windows, and bowls of spicy stew. "Once upon a time," we'll tell them. We're sure the babies will listen.

SLEEPING WITH ACHE

Last night I slept with Ache. And I will again tonight and tomorrow. I keep track. I mark the calendar, a big X for every night with Ache. A month, then two. Rain or shine. But here's the good news: Ache doesn't snore, never wraps a sweaty arm around me, insists I talk about this and that, the before and after of us. Ache is just there, like the old dog curled nose to tail in the middle of the bed, in a pocket of quilt and incoming dark. I could say Ache don't come. Stay downstairs, on the couch. No need to turn the TV off. Let it blare. I hardly sleep and only remember one dream anyway. I'm sitting in a barrel of ice water. My hands are chafed. I'm fat. Tired. Tonight I will tell my husband that Ache is here between us. He will crack the bottom window for air, turn back the sheet.

SONG

One horse is humming a little horse song. We might say this horse is fat and happy, point to wet dapples and mane, undo a top button. The other horse is dead. Once a branch broke just before midnight. Once two brothers pressed their cheeks against frozen pond, giggling. It was November, no wind, no birds, no moment of sky. We think this horse is humming about branches and runaway boys in flannel caps, but we don't ask. The other horse is dead. It grazed nearby, stretched its neck for clover. And now this horse is humming a little horse song. Perhaps a simple song, short but lovely, or a song for thrashing hooves, the certain coming of grief. We might sit on a fence and convince ourselves that if horses don't want to remember, they won't. They will close their eyes, stand rump to rump, share only sunlight or shadow.

BAG STORY

Scissors, green wool tights, a pound of orange and lemon Chuckles. Say you put these in your bag. Say you throw it over your shoulder, walk up and down the block, stop only at one hour meters to check your breath. Don't let them look. Not even the pudgy white boy dreaming of Barbie doll breasts. Your bag, you tell yourself, your bag. Say two sisters, Edna and Dorothy, flag you down. Twirling their hair into tight blonde ringlets, they try to reach inside your bag. Say a butcher hangs out a window, promises pig knuckles and extra salt if he could feel its edges, maybe try to buy it. Say they all have a meeting, drink some coffee and name it something fancy, like satchel, tote, or attaché. Don't let them near it. Your bag, you tell yourself, your bag. Not even a zipper. Wave goodbye.

ON THE DAY I SAY GOODBYE TO ACHE

Should I stand on my porch, wearing boots and a blue chenille robe? Should I wave and look forlornly, thinking I could have fried some eggs, cooked up a heap of bacon—a last hearty breakfast for the road? If it's Monday or Wednesday, foggy with no real birds in the forecast, that's what I'll do. I'll sigh, pour tea as if for a friend. Reach across the tablecloth. Or should I scribble a few choice words, a note perhaps, short yet emphatic? Should I use thin crinkled paper or carve each letter into the doorframe, the floorboards, down the middle of the banister? If it's Thursday, I'll begin early. I'll sit alone, sharpening a knife. Or should I just wish for claws? The kind that rip and shred too easily. Should I open my chest, tearing and taking until I find that spot, oh, that little red spot? Should I wait before I lift my head and flap my hollow wings?

A BIRD OF UNDETERMINED PROPORTIONS

Wings opened, full bodysuit of feathers, red-trimmed eyes and chiseled bird cheeks.

The horse is taller at the withers, its tail much like a giant plume of weather. The barn cat and beagles are eager, but smaller in breadth. I'm working hard not to confuse breadth with breath.

The bird is a presence. Self-contained, unrestrained aviary. I take more notes, meticulous scribbles up and down the inside of my forearm: scattering of sunflower seeds, bony feet perched on the lawn chair, profile of beak in partial sun under the arch of forsythia. How did it get there to here? How did we get here to there?

Come nightfall, I'm growing tired of the bird. It picks its way closer, taking up space. I'm thinking nest, far away, my front yard free of all sorts and song.

PSALM

Cats of paper and pencil. Cats deep in embryonic thought. Cats who write only on Mondays and always begin with bladder. *Bladder this and bladder that.* Then they turn the page.

I watch them. Beseechingly, I stand behind them. May I stick my fingers down their throats? May I squeeze their inner truths until I'm faint? Let me do this in the name of envy, before I bow my head, before I bind my hands, thumb over thumb, in reams of thistle.

Cats of obsequious margins. Cats with middle initials and big snappy verbs. Cats who never swear. Instead they press down hard. *Isn't it sadder that the food is badder.* A puddle of drool and the gray one growing plump and moody, like Kafka on his wooden stool.

Let's not pretend. They sharpen their pencils. Lords of lead and petty anecdotes: a butcher, a resurrection, an island slapped silly by belligerent tides. May I kneel in the shadow of cats, may crows bounce off my forehead.

It's true. I've called them names, made unbecoming noises, imagined their tails tucked deep inside them. I am shameful. All of me. Forgive my fingers. Forgive my desire.

ACKNOWLEDGMENTS

Grateful acknowledgment is made to the following journals where some of these poems have appeared.

The Denver Quarterly: "The Lake Shore Limited," "Vigil"

The Illinois Review: "Simple as This Night," "Come Back, Elvis, Come Back to Holyoke," "Red Door"

Key Satch (EL): "Norma Nelson Finds Her Heaven," "The Farmer's Way," "Falling," "Lake and Michigan"

The Journal: "Talk," "Tree Man," "The Headache," "How I Find Ache Everywhere," "Naming Ache"

The Laurel Review: "On Weeping Icons," "On the 50th Anniversary of D Day Stella Longs for Love"

The Massachusetts Review: "Bless This Night," "Love Poem"

The Prose Poem: An International Journal: "After the Weather," "Emanuel on the Tightrope," "The Big, Deep Voice of God," "Dead Horse," "Psalm"

Sentence: A Journal of Prose Poems: "Maybe It's Still Winter"

The Sycamore Review: "Erma Jacowitts Pleads Her Case"

Tarpaulin Sky: "When the Babies Discover Torque," "When the Babies Read *The Book of the Dead*"

three candles: "Sideswiping the Pig," "Blackflies," "Something Like the Earth"

"Red Door" was reprinted in *Crossing Paths: An Anthology of Poems by Women.*

"The Big, Deep Voice of God" was reprinted in *Ladies, Start Your Engines: Women Writing on Cars and the Road.*

"The Year of the Man," "The Second Song of Insomnia," and "Come Back, Elvis, Come Back to Holyoke" appeared in *The Party Train: A Collection of North American Prose Poetry.*

The following poems were included in *No Boundaries, Prose Poems by 24 Prose Poets:* "The Lake Shore Limited," "Come Back, Elvis, Come Back to Holyoke," "Bump," "On Weeping Icons," "Love Poem," "The Year of the Man," "Meditation on a Bird Sitting on a Man's Head," "When the Babies Are Missing Again," and "The Second Song of Insomnia."

"Come Back, Elvis, Come Back to Holyoke" was reprinted in *Real Things: An Anthology of Popular Culture in American Poetry*.

"Love Poem" and "Erma Jacowitts Pleads Her Case" were reprinted in *This Wood Sang Out*.

"Norma Nelson Finds Her Heaven" was reprinted in *Poetry Daily*.

Several of these poems appeared in *Closer to Day*, a chapbook of this author's work published by Quale Press.

I'd like to thank the Massachusetts Cultural Council for its generous support.

Many thanks to Debra Carney, Margaret Szumowski, and Carol Fetler for their endless wisdom, humor, and patience.

And more thanks to Lee Upton, Ellen Watson, Carol Potter, Amy Dryansky, and Ann Boutelle; the members of my First Thursday Night of the Month Writing Group; and my prose poem buddies—Peter Johnson and Gian Lombardo—for all their insights and encouragement.

The text of this book is set in ten point ITC Galliard, designed in 1978 by Matthew Carter for Merganthaler, and is a close reinterpretation of the originals of Robert Granjon. A 16th century French printer, publisher and letter cutter, Granjon's typefaces were reknowned for their beauty and legibility, particularly his italics.